WOODLAND PEOPLE, DESERT PEOPLE

Jaqueline D. Greene

S0-BEF-222

Contents

Can You Imagine?................................2

Woodland Homes 4

Desert Homes....................................10

Woodland Clothing.............................14

Desert Clothing..................................16

Woodland Food..................................17

Desert Food 19

Woodland People, Desert People..............23

Index...24

Rigby
A Harcourt Achieve Imprint

www.Rigby.com
1-800-531-5015

Can You Imagine?

It's hard to imagine what life was like for Native Americans 400 years ago. Could you spend a snowy winter living in a house made of tree bark? Could you run barefoot for hours every day to fill jugs of water for your family?

If you had lived with the Chippewa in the northern woodlands near the Great Lakes, you would have learned how to survive in the harsh, snowy winters. If you had lived with the Tohono O'odham (toe-HOE-no-aw-aw-TAM) in the southwest desert, you would have learned how to survive in the dry, hot summers with little water.

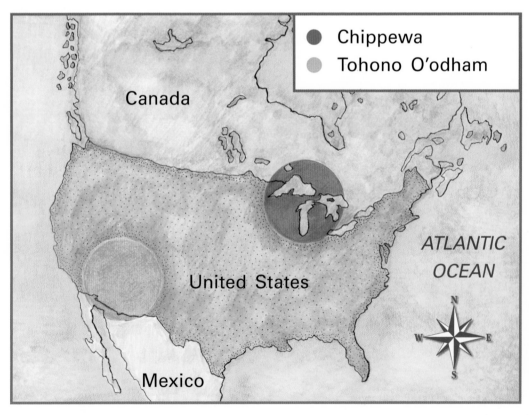

Woodland Homes

In the 1600s, French fur traders landed in North America and met the Chippewa people. All around were rivers, lakes, and deep forests. The traders were amazed to see that the Chippewa used trees and bark to build round homes called wigwams. These simple houses kept them warm all winter and could be moved easily.

The Chippewa lived in wigwams like this one.

Young trees were bent to form a dome for each wigwam.

To make a wigwam, boys helped their fathers cut young trees called saplings. They bent the trees to make a frame shaped like a dome. Then women carefully covered it with strips of bark. In winter they added an extra layer to keep the wigwam warmer. An animal skin hung over the doorway, which could be left open or closed, depending on the weather.

Inside the wigwam, the Chippewa dug a fire pit in the center of the dirt floor. In winter they made the pit deeper to burn bigger logs. It could get smoky inside, so a hole in the roof helped smoke escape. A fire had to be kept burning all the time for light, cooking, and heat.

Sometimes a pipe was added to carry smoke out of the hole in the wigwam's roof.

Women wove floor mats from rushes, a type of tall grass that grows near lakes and rivers. The mats helped keep the floor clean and made the wigwam warmer. At night the families slept on deer hides or bearskins near the fire. When it was especially cold, they snuggled under an extra animal skin blanket.

Chippewa women wove large grass mats from dried rushes.

Each morning women hung the animal skin blankets outside in the fresh air. Then they rolled them up and pushed them against the walls of the wigwam. The rolled blankets helped keep cold air out and gave people a comfortable place to sit.

Animal skin blankets were hung outside in the fresh air each morning.

When it was time to move to a new site, the Chippewa rolled up the strips of bark that covered the wigwam. They took down the frame. Then they tied the house poles together with the bark on top. Older children pulled them along as they walked. When the families arrived at a new location, they built their wigwam again in a few hours.

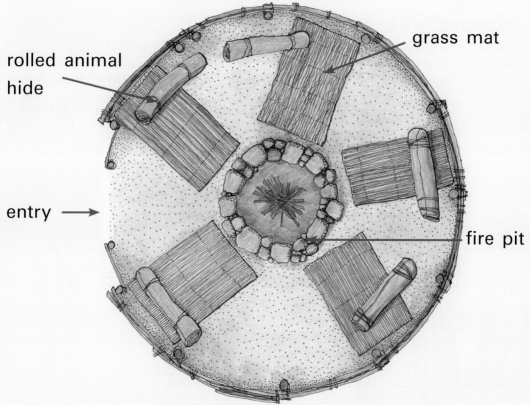

rolled animal hide

grass mat

entry →

fire pit

Desert Homes

The name Tohono O'odham means Desert People. This group lived in the Southwest, in what is now Arizona and Mexico. When Spanish explorers arrived in the 1500s, the Desert People lived in homes that were also shaped like round domes. But there weren't many trees in the desert, so they built their homes with cactuses.

When this cactus dies, it leaves behind strong ribs that can be used to build houses.

The walls made of dry brush let in light and let out smoke.

The Desert People cut tall, thin cactuses and placed them in the sandy ground. They covered the frame with dry brush or small sticks. Years later, after they saw Spanish-style buildings, they built square houses with flat roofs covered with grass or sticks. The roofs didn't need a smoke hole, since there were spaces in the walls and an open doorway.

In the center of the main house, a fire pit provided light and gave heat on cool winter nights. The family slept on woven grass mats. They didn't use blankets, but slept close to the fire on chilly desert nights.

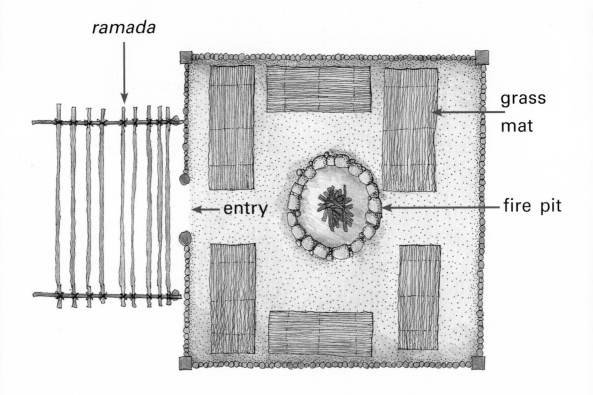

ramada

grass mat

entry

fire pit

An open *ramada* connected to each house made a cool, shady place to work and sleep.

Along the north side of the house, the family built a shaded area called a *ramada*. The top was covered with sticks, and there were no walls. This was a cool place to stay out of the sun for working, cooking, and sleeping. Pots and baskets could be stored under the *ramada*, as well as clay jugs filled with cool water.

Woodland Clothing

Chippewa women made clothes from animal hides. Thread was made from plants or animals, and needles were made out of bone. The whole family worked hard scraping animal skins clean. Then they would dry them on a wooden frame.

Men and boys wore buckskin shirts and leggings, and women and girls wore deerskin dresses. Their clothes were beautifully decorated with dyed porcupine quills, shells, or colorful beads.

Chippewa women decorated clothes with colorful designs, like the ones worn by this dancer.

How Did the Chippewa Prepare Animal Hides?

- Men skinned an animal.
- Women and girls cleaned the hide with a bone scraper.
- Families stretched the skin on a wood frame.
- Women rubbed oils into the skin to make it soft and waterproof.
- The skin was left out to dry over a smoky fire.

Everyone in the Chippewa tribe wore deerskin moccasins on their feet. Moccasins wore out quickly, and women were always making new pairs. In winter the Chippewa lined their moccasins with rabbit or squirrel fur for extra warmth.

Fur-lined moccasins kept the Chippewa's feet warm in cold weather.

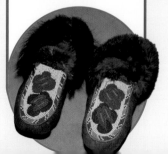

Desert Clothing

Before the Spanish arrived, the Tohono O'odham wore very little clothing because it was so hot. They almost always went barefoot. After the Spanish settled nearby, women wove cotton cloth and sewed shirts, pants, and dresses. The light cotton clothing helped the Desert people stay cooler in the heat.

Tohono O'odham women wove dresses out of cotton.

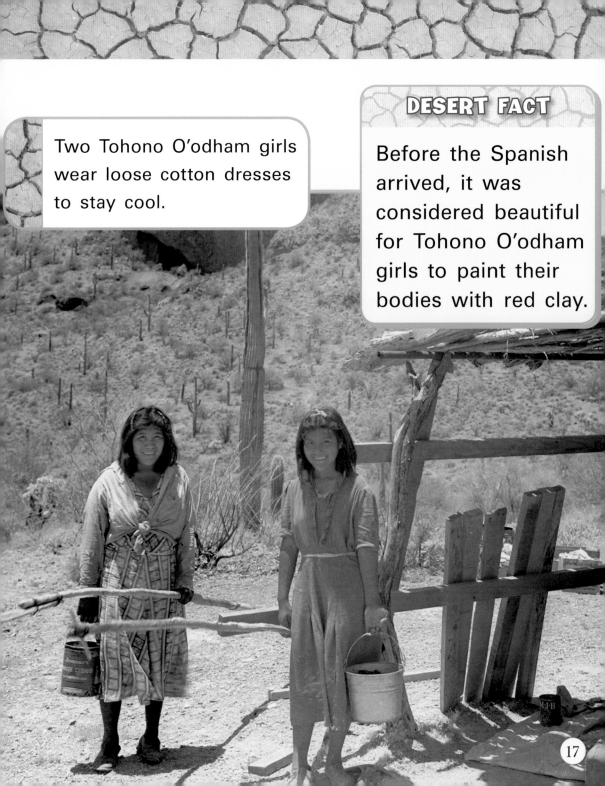

Two Tohono O'odham girls wear loose cotton dresses to stay cool.

Before the Spanish arrived, it was considered beautiful for Tohono O'odham girls to paint their bodies with red clay.

Woodland Cooking

The forest had many animals that the Chippewa could hunt for meat. There were rabbits, squirrels, deer, moose, and bears. They also loved to go fishing. Meat and fish could be dried over a smoky fire and stored until winter. When the lakes would freeze and it was too cold for hunting, the Chippewa needed the dried food.

WOODLAND FACT

There were no set mealtimes, so the Chippewa ate whenever they felt hungry.

Chippewa families moved to maple tree groves in early spring and collected buckets of sap. They boiled it until the syrup could be shaped into hard sugar balls. This maple sugar was stored and used to flavor food. In summer they grew squash, beans, corn, and potatoes. They picked wild berries and nuts. When autumn came, they camped near shallow lakes and harvested wild rice that grew there.

Today Chippewa still paddle the lakes in their birch bark canoes to collect wild rice.

Desert Cooking

Like the Chippewa, the Tohono O'odham also moved around as the seasons changed. But food on the desert was very different. There wasn't much water. Each morning before dawn, girls traveled long distances to collect enough water for the day. Clay water jugs hung under the shady *ramada.*

Girls traveled for hours to mountain streams, carrying two clay jugs in a net backpack. They had to be careful not to break the jugs or spill even a drop of water.

DESERT FACT

For the Tohono O'odham, it was polite to offer visitors a precious drink of water.

In spring the Tohono O'odham picked ripe cactus fruit. Some kinds of fruit were cooked into syrup to make a sweet drink, while others were roasted. The spring felt like a holiday as many families came together to work, play, and feast.

How Did the Tohono O'odham Prepare a Cholla Cactus?

- First they picked off the buds with wooden tongs.
- Next they rolled the buds in sand to remove all the thorns.
- Finally they roasted the buds overnight in a pit of hot coals.

When the temperatures reached as high as 110 degrees Fahrenheit in the desert, the families moved. They went to the cool mountains where they could hunt animals such as antelope, bighorn sheep, and deer. There were also many plants and trees in the mountains, so they collected acorns, pine nuts, bean pods, wild chili peppers, and onions.

When the vegetables were ripe, Tohono O'odham families returned to the deserts to pick them. Many vegetables were eaten fresh, but some were dried and stored for the winter.

Tohono O'odham people collected bean pods to eat.

Woodland People, Desert People

If you had lived with woodland people or desert people, some things would be the same. Your home would keep you safe from the weather. You'd make comfortable clothes. And you'd learn how to find, grow, cook, and store food. Most of all, you would learn to live in the climate, so you'd never feel too hot or too cold!

Index

cactus 10–11, 17, 21

Chippewa 3–9, 14–15, 18–19

clothes 14–17

food 18–22

moccasins 15

ramada 11, 13, 20

Tohono O'odham 3, 10–13,
    16–17, 20–22

wigwams 4–9, 18